The Amazing Musical Magical Plants

Story by Thornton Cline and Crystal Bowman
Illustrations by Susan Oliver

ISBN: 978-1-57424-325-3
SAN 683-8022

Cover by James Creative Group

All Illustrations by Susan Oliver

"Crystal Bowman and Thornton Cline have imaginatively captured the connection between practice and musical growth—whether that be plants growing before the very eyes of practicing students or the superior sound of the band! The rousing climax will delight and entertain all."

– Nancy and Randall Faber, co-authors of Piano Adventures

'The "Amazing Magical Musical Plants" is a cute story young students will enjoy and also learn from. This book has a CD of musical samples included to enhance the story's learning experience. Parents and teachers alike will appreciate the message explaining the virtues of practice and patience, as well as the future rewards of doing so.'

– Pattie Cossentino, Nashville Saxophone Artist and Multi-Instrumentalist

"The Amazing Magical Musical Plants" is a delightful book that will appeal to children, parents, and teachers alike. This clever story is enhanced by fascinating artwork, making for an engaging and memorable reading experience.

– Keith Christopher, Composer/Author

The Amazing Magical Musical Plants" immediately tweaks one's curiosity and is a compelling read, being both entertaining and inspiring - encouraging children to practice and spend time with their instruments. Playing a musical instrument is such a beautiful activity for children - it trains and improves focus, while improving general well-being as well. Any book that encourages children to play and practise is an investment into their future.

– Wouter Kellerman, Flutist & Composer, Grammy® Award Winner (2015), Billboard No. 1 Artist and 5-time SAMA (South African Music Award) Winner

Music Education and Thornton Cline have become synonymous. In "The Amazing Magical Musical Plants" he has captured the joy and wonder of music through the eyes of a child. Bravo Thornton!"

– Karl B. Sanger, Sanger Talent Agency & Music Unlimited

"This is a cute story that will motivate students to practice, and also enhance music instrument recognition. It is beautifully illustrated, and would have much appeal to young musicians"

– Glenn Martin, Nashville Trombone Artist and Composer

Once again author and music teacher Thornton Cline comes up with a fantastic and intelligent way to inspire and encourage students to practice. His new book, "The Amazing Magical Musical Plants" is not only a fun lighthearted read for young music students, it teaches music educators to think outside of the box when coming up with ways to get their younger students to practice. Thanks Thornton!

– Bart Robley, Professional drummer, drum set educator, clinician and author

Music has the ability to transcend and affect everything. This is a nicely written and illustrated book that can help to motivate the music student to hopefully practice. With practice comes improvement and confidence with the end result being beautiful art.

– Jerry Tachoir, Grammy-nominated Contemporary jazz mallet artist/clinician

The Amazing Musical Magical Plants

Mr. Jones was the fifth grade band teacher at Jack and Iris's school. He had no hair because it was all shaved off. He wore his favorite brown plaid sports coat with a yellow bow tie and carried his large conductor's baton.

Jack played the flute and Iris played the clarinet in Mr. Jones's band. He often made his students laugh. But lately he was not very happy.

"I need to get my students excited about practicing," Mr. Jones said.

He looked around his house in search of something to help. He soon discovered an old trombone he had bought at an antique store. He looked inside the case and found a packet of seeds with instructions on how to grow Amazing Magical Musical Plants.

"I wonder if this will work," said Mr. Jones. He decided to find out. Mr. Jones filled twenty pots with soil. Then he planted a seed in each pot. The next day he brought the pots to school.

"I have something for each of you," Mr. Jones told his students. "I found some seeds and planted one in each of these pots. Take one home and give your seed plenty of sunlight and water. But most importantly, play your instrument every day. Then the seed will grow into a plant."

The students laughed at the notion of playing their instruments for a pot of soil. "What kinds of plants are these?" Iris asked.

"I'm not sure," said Mr. Jones. "The packet said Amazing Magical Musical Plants."

"So if we play our instruments will the seed grow into a plant?" Jack asked.

"Yes. And the more you play the faster the plant will grow," Mr. Jones replied.

The boys in the trombone section in the back of the room laughed and said, "You must be kidding us."

But Mr. Jones was not kidding.

When the bell rang at the end of class, most of the students took a pot of soil. A few of the doubting students left their pots at school and forgot about them.

Weeks passed and the students didn't see any plants growing.

"I play every day for the seed in my pot, but no plant is coming up yet," Jack said.

"I play my clarinet, water the soil, and give my seed plenty of sunlight, but I don't see a plant either. Are you sure you put a seed in the pot?" Iris asked.

The band students laughed and decided it was a joke played on them by Mr. Jones.

"Have patience and keep on practicing," Mr. Jones said.

On Monday morning Iris rushed into class. "My plant is growing!" she said.

"So is mine!" said Jack.

Many of the students were excited that their plants were starting to grow. And Mr. Jones was excited because the band was starting to sound pretty good from all the practicing—except for the trombone players who were playing the wrong notes and were horribly out of tune.

"Have you been practicing?" Mr. Jones asked them. They shrugged their shoulders and didn't answer.

Mr. Jones found three dried up pots in the back of the room behind the tuba cases.

"Who didn't bring their pots home?" he asked as he looked at the trombone players.

They shrugged their shoulders again. No one in the room admitted to leaving their pots at school.

"Well, there's one way to find out," said Mr. Jones. "For the rest of the week, practice your instruments as often as you can. On Friday bring your plants to school. Then we will see who has the tallest and biggest plant."

Jack and Iris practiced three times a day for the rest of the week. Many of the other students practiced too.

The trombone players took their pots home when no one was looking. The soil was all dried up, but they hoped if they watered their seeds, gave them sunlight and practiced every day, their plants would grow. So that is what they did. They practiced after school and after supper. They practiced way past their bedtime. But all they had were pots of soil.

On Friday the students brought their plants to the band room to show Mr. Jones.

"I see who has been practicing," he said. Good job, Jack and Iris. Your plants are tall and thick. You must have practiced every day."

"Yes we did," they said.

Mr. Jones walked around the room and looked at the plants. Some were medium and some were a bit smaller. But he could see that everyone had been practicing.

He looked at the trombone players.

"May I see your pots?" he asked

The three boys showed Mr. Jones their pots.

"You've haven't been practicing," he said.

"We thought it was a joke," said one boy.

"We practiced hard this week," said another.

"Let me hear you play," said Mr. Jones.

The three boys held up their trombones and began to play.

The more they played the better they sounded.

"Look!" said Iris as she pointed to three pots.

The soil split apart as little green sprouts popped out from below.

"Keep playing!" everyone shouted.

The boys kept playing and the sprouts kept growing—right before their eyes!

The students were excited that all of the seeds finally grew into Amazing Magical Musical Plants. And Mr. Jones was excited too because his whole band sounded great—even the trombone section.

THE END.

Can playing music really make plants grow faster and taller?

Some people think so. Several studies have been done through the years and people have found that it depends on the kind of music being played and the types of plants used in the experiment. Some plants grew faster with classical music and jazz. Plants don't really "hear" the music. What they respond to is the vibrations from the sound waves that they can feel.

Do you think music can make plants grow faster? Why don't you try it and find out!

Song Titles

CD Track List

1. The Amazing Magical Musical Plants
   (narration by Jayla Palma)

2. The Amazing Magical Musical Plants
   (narration by Jayla Palma with page turn
   tones)

Children's solo songs with piano and instrument

3. The Flute
4. The Clarinet
5. The Oboe
6. The Saxophone
7. The Trumpet
8. The French Horn
9. The Bassoon
10. The Trombone
11. The Tuba
12. The Drum

The Flute

Crystal Bowman and Thornton Cline

Lyrics under the music:

The flute plays high and high - er_____.

Hold it up to the right side of you_____.

Press the keys, blow till you get a pret - ty sound.

The flute is shi - ny and sil - ver too_____.

Hold it up, to the right side of you.

The Clarinet

Crystal Bowman and Thornton Cline

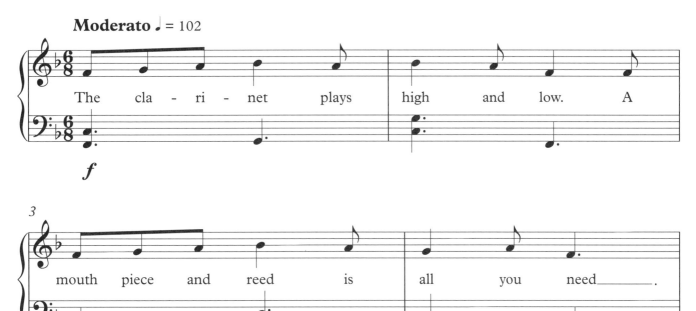

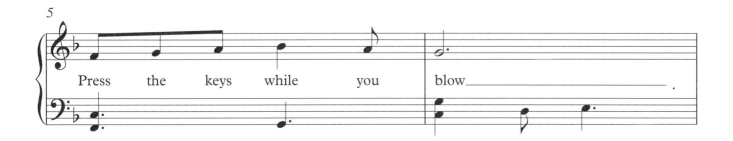

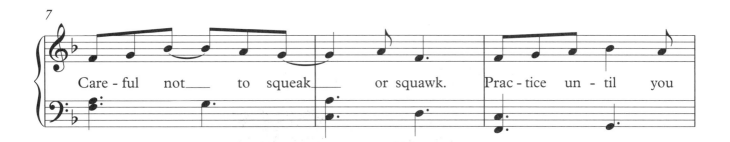

The Oboe

Crystal Bowman and Thornton Cline

Moderato ♩ = 104

mf The o - boe's long and thin, much like the cla - ri - net. It has two reeds you can blow_____ . A mel - low sound's what you get. Press the keys, don't be shy. I know you can do it if you try.

The Saxophone

Crystal Bowman and Thornton Cline

The Trumpet

Crystal Bowman and Thornton Cline

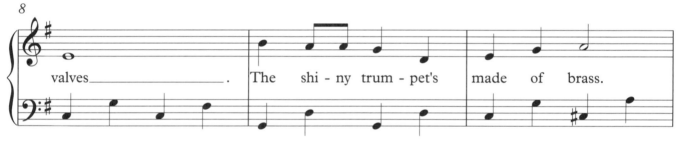

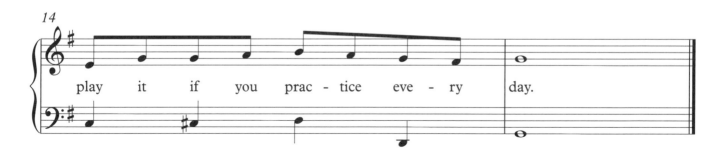

The French Horn

Crystal Bowman and Thornton Cline

The Bassoon

Crystal Bowman and Thornton Cline

Moderato ♩ = 102

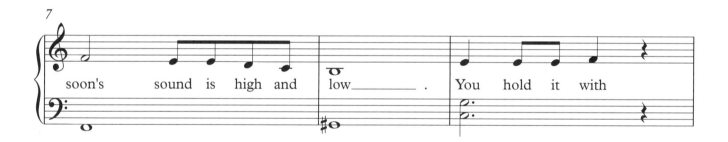

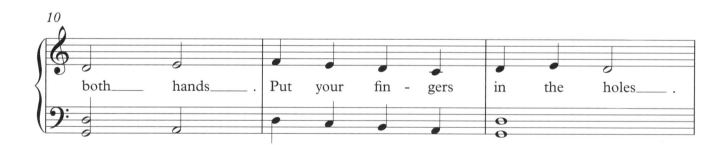

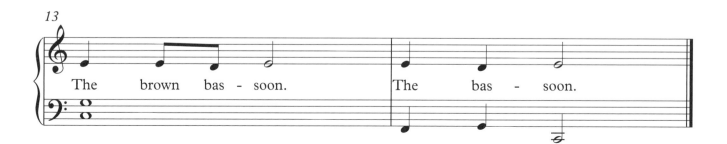

The Trombone

Crystal Bowman and Thornton Cline

March ♩ = 108

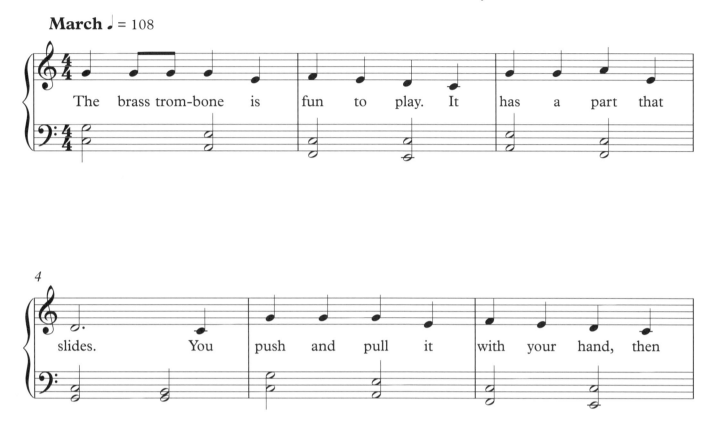

The brass trom-bone is fun to play. It has a part that

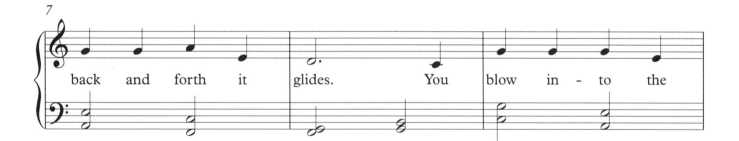

slides. You push and pull it with your hand, then

back and forth it glides. You blow in - to the

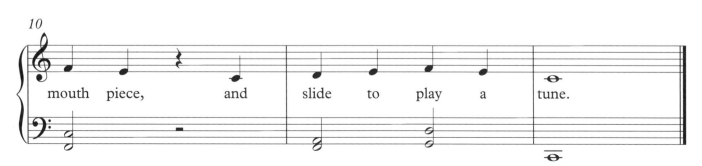

mouth piece, and slide to play a tune.

The Tuba

Crystal Bowman and Thornton Cline

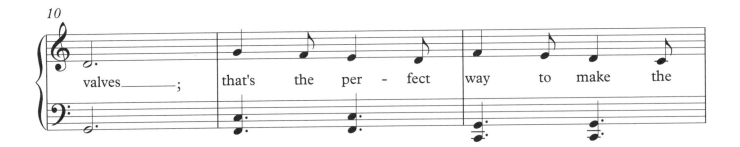

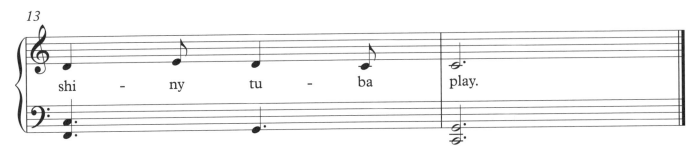

The Drum

Crystal Bowman and Thornton Cline

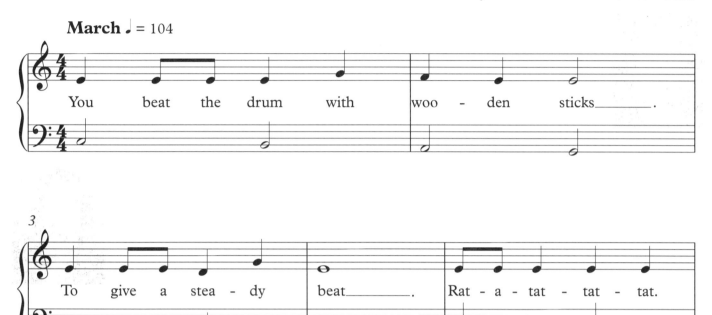

Biographies

Thornton Cline is a bestselling author of seven books. Cline has been honored with Songwriter of the Year twice in a row for his hit song, "Love Is the Reason." Cline has received Dove Award and Grammy Award nominations. Cline is an in-demand author, teacher, speaker, clinician, musician and songwriter. He lives in Hendersonville, Tennessee with his wife and children.

Crystal Bowman is a bestselling, award-winning author of over 100 books for children. She also writes stories for kid's magazines and lyrics for children's piano music. Her songs can be found in the *Piano Adventure* series by Faber and Faber. She enjoys writing humorous poems for children and teaching writing workshops in the classroom. Her books have been translated into many different languages. Crystal lives in Florida with her husband and enjoys spending time with her grandchildren.

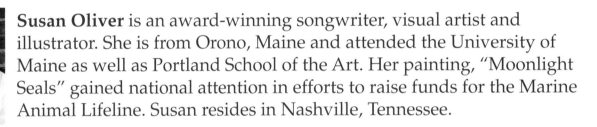

Susan Oliver is an award-winning songwriter, visual artist and illustrator. She is from Orono, Maine and attended the University of Maine as well as Portland School of the Art. Her painting, "Moonlight Seals" gained national attention in efforts to raise funds for the Marine Animal Lifeline. Susan resides in Nashville, Tennessee.

Jayla Palmer, at 16 years old, is an experienced stage and screen actress. She has appeared in many feature films, short films, music videos, commercials, and stage productions. She also runs a blog, www. justbeingjayla.com as well as a YouTube channel, where she makes videos and written content that show off her fun and affable personality. Website: www.jaylapalmer.com.

Libby has been involved in a variety of musical productions and plays the violin. She is the youngest of eight children, loves animals, enjoys her friends, and the great outdoors. Her hometown is Nashville, Tennessee.

Ethan is a seventh grader who enjoys singing, beat-boxing, acting and playing sports. He is a straight A student and a native of the Tennessee. In his free time, he enjoys playing video games and spending time with his friends and family. Ethan is very excited about being a part of this musical project.

Credits

Audrey Cline

Alex Cline

Mollie Cline

God

Ron Middlebrook

Clinetel Music

Centerstream Publishing

Hal Leonard

Susan Oliver

Jayla Palmer

Libby P.

Ethan K.

Todd Taylor

Marcelo Cataldo

Parents of children

Sumner Academy

Cumberland Arts Academy

Cumberland University

Hendersonville Christian Academy

Gallatin Creative Arts Center

Jonathan Edwards Classical Academy

More Amazing Books!

THE AMAZING INCREDIBLE SHRINKING VIOLIN

Story by Thornton Cline, Illustrations by Susan Oliver

Young Austin begs his parents to play violin. But Austin doesn't make time to practice until one night he is visited by the violin fairy who warns him that if he doesn't practice his violin, it will shrink. Austin's classmates are amazed at what happens next! Austin discovers that if he wants to sound good, he must practice. This heartwarming story teaches the benefits of hard work and attaining one's goals. Austin's dream of becoming a big violin star is starting to come true. The book's whimsical illustrations by acclaimed illustrator Susan Oliver add to the charm and merriment of the story. The book includes a CD of 10 easy original songs for violin or voice (with lyrics sung by a children's choir) and narrations of the story. (Recommended for ages 4-8)

00142509 Book/CD Pack.................................$19.99

THE AMAZING INCREDIBLE SHRINKING PIANO

Story by Thornton Cline, Illustrations by Susan Oliver

Lily is given a piano from her grandmother for her birthday. Lily continues to slam her hands against the keys with anger when she makes mistakes. One night she is visited by her grandmother in a dream who warns Lily not to hit her piano anymore or it will shrink. Lily discovers the secret of how to keep her piano from shrinking. This heartwarming story teaches the respect of the piano. Lily learns how to play beautiful music on her piano without hitting her piano keys. The whimsical illustrations by acclaimed illustrator Susan Oliver add to the charm and merriment of the story. The book includes a CD of 10 easy original songs for piano or voice (with lyrics sung by a children's choir) and narrations of the story. (Recommended for ages 4-8)

00149098 Book/CD Pack.................................$19.99

P.O. Box 17878 - Anaheim Hills, CA 92817

(714) 779-9390   www.centerstream-usa.com

More Great Books from Thornton Cline...

PRACTICE PERSONALITIES: WHAT'S YOUR TYPE?
Identifying and Understanding the Practice Personality Type in the Music Student
by Thornton Cline
Teaching is one of the greatest responsibilities in society. It's an art form that requires craft, patience, creativity, and intelligence. Practice Personalities: What's Your Type? will help teachers, parents and students realize the challenges of practicing, understand the benefits of correct practicing, identify and understand nine practice personality types, and employ useful strategies to effectively motivate and inspire each type of student. The accompanying CD demonstrates effective practice strategies for selected piano, violin and guitar excerpts from the book.

00101974 Book/CD Pack $24.99

Companion DVD Available
00121577 DVD $19.99

PRACTICE PERSONALITIES FOR ADULTS
Identifying and Understanding the Practice Personality Type in the Adult Music Student
by Thornton Cline
Did you know that your personality can affect the way you learn and perform on a musical instrument? This book identifies nine practice personalities in music students. Adults will learn how to practice more effectively and efficiently according to their personalities. A Practice Personalities test is included along with an accompanying CD.
00131613 Book/CD Pack $24.99

P.O. Box 17878 - Anaheim Hills, CA 92817
(714) 779-9390   www.centerstream-usa.com

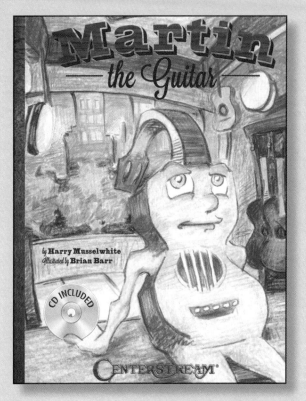